WHY DOES SHE ALWAYS TALK ABOUT HER HUSBAND?

Poems by David Romanda

BLUE
CEDAR
PRESS

Wichita, Kansas

WHY DOES SHE ALWAYS TALK ABOUT HER HUSBAND?

Blue Cedar Press
PO Box 48715
Wichita, KS 67201
Visit the Blue Cedar Press website: https://bluecedarpress.com

First edition November 2022

10 9 8 7 6 5 4 3 2 1

ISBN: 978-1-958728-07-9 (ebook)

ISBN: 978-1-958728-06-2 (paper)

Library of Congress Control Number (LCCN): 2022947139

Cover design by Gretchen Eick

Interior layout by Gina Laiso

Printed by IngramSpark in the US and abroad

To Atsuko

Contents

Freckles

I'll remember
the wash of freckles
across Debby's forehead
& across the bridge
of her nose
I'll remember
the freckles that spill
from her shoulders
to her forearms
to the backs of her hands
with slight veins snaking
under pale skin
I'll remember
the spattered freckles
over her chest
& her ever bud-tiny breasts
I'll remember
the few freckles dripped
on Debby's pink knees
& the few dropped
at her lily-cool ankles
I'll remember
the freckles splashed
around her thorny Christ tattoo
the one you need to slip off her panties to see

Dad

He sat me down.
I was nine
and a half.
It seemed like
he'd been crying.
There was crust
in the corner of his mouth.
"I've got cancer
in my throat," he told me.
All these years later,
I remember the crust
in the corner of his mouth.

Tina Says

Before I sleep with you
I need to look through your wallet
and check your sock drawer.
You can watch—I just need to be sure
that you are who you say you are.

Home

You get home after a long day at the rat race
And you find a giant wife-sized rat in the kitchen
The rat's cutting a lasagna
The rat says: "Welcome home, honey"
He's wearing your wife's "Caution:
Extremely Hot" apron
(It's a little tight, but it fits)
The rat's smoking one of your cigars
Through the smells of lasagna and cigar
You can smell your wife's perfume
(The rat's wearing your wife's perfume)
The rat says: "Sit down, baby,
Poor thing,
You must be exhausted"
You sit down

What Lasts

Like they say,
What lasts is what
You start with.
And what you start with
Is a sort of longing.
A longing for God
Knows what.

Jurassic Park

I begged Grandma to buy me a Velociraptor action figure
(the dinosaur with that killer razor-toe claw thing). Grandmas
are good because sooner or later they buy you what you want.
Then Grandpa took me up fishing. I went for a walk
with my action figure. If you pulled back the legs, it screeched
It was pretty impressive. I was walking across a field, not far
from where Grandpa was setting up camp, and there before me
was a family of deer. A big one with medium sized antlers and
another big one without antlers and two small ones. They looked
at me, but the one with antlers really looked. I held up my Velociraptor
I wasn't scared, I just held him up for some reason. Maybe ten seconds
passed. It felt like a long time. And then I just, don't ask me why,
I pulled the dinosaur's legs back and it screeched way out loud
The deer scattered. They were gone.

Longevity

You
won't give up
even after

you
no longer
want the prize

Spring Break

Me and Tim Zorno
were playing tennis.
We were equally
bad players,
and we both
desperately wanted
to win.
We played
most mornings
over that three-week
spring break.
One day some
older kids came
when we were
in the middle of a game.
They just watched us.
We stopped playing.
The tennis courts
were fenced in.
Three of them
entered and the others
blocked both
metal-framed doors
from the outside.
Tim went
over to the far door.
I stood there
with my racket
down by my side.
The three boys
approached.
I looked around,

but nobody was there
to see any trouble
or hear any screaming
(if it came to that).
I was scared, but I knew
I had to ride it out.
I didn't look at Tim.
I looked at
the biggest kid.
He stepped forward.
He wore a black hoody
even though
it was sunny and hot.
His eyes were mean.
He opened a knife.
He was doing these
tricks with the knife,
little spins,
practiced movements,
controlled,
switching from hand
to hand.
He was four feet
in front of me.
He said nothing,
I said nothing.
Everyone was quiet.
I held my racket
down by my side.
I didn't think
to pray
(afterwards,
I thought
that was kind of cool).

I was just
riding it out.
There was nothing
else to do.
And then the knife
was gone.
The big kid
in the hoody said,
"Come on!
Let's get the fuck outta here."
They were gone.

the greed of weeds?

weeds are beautiful
let them crack up the sidewalk

tadpoles

does she spit
you in
the sink?
or in
the toilet?

which do
you prefer?

Wrong

He married
the wrong woman

He admits to marrying
the wrong woman

He continues making a life with
the wrong woman

Nikki

I was dating the flower shop clown girl.
They had her stand in front of the shop
along that busy road holding a sign that
said Daisies. She wore a curly rainbow
colored wig, had the white clown makeup,
the round red cheeks, and that squishy
red nose. Her one-piece outfit was yellow
with white polka dots. For six months
she was my girl. A few months before we
broke up, they fitted me in some extra clown
gear and I joined her outside the flower shop.
There we were in the sunlight, laughing,
holding hands (the Daisies sign propped up
against a bucket), waving at the passing cars.

cactus juice

i kinda hoped
it would change my life

Golden Ticket

The golden ticket for a poet is getting cancer.
The death of a parent is a golden ticket.
Divorce, too. You get the idea.
You'll make it through.

Contact

This guy on the bus started talking to me. He told me
he was writing a book. Here we go, I thought.
But I was in a good mood and asked him what
the book was about. He gave me some perplexing
name for some psychological phenomena or theory or
something. I looked confused. It's about relationships,
he said. About breakups. If she leaves you, you don't
make contact, he said. (He was looking me intensely
in the eyes. We were sitting beside each other on the bus.)
She leaves, and you don't beg. You don't call her.
You don't try to find her. You wait. You wait however
long it takes. When she makes contact, when she's ready,
then you talk things out. Then you get back together, he said.
Then my stop came. I got up. That's the book, he said.
Thanks, I said. And I got off the bus.

The End is the Beginning is the End

We fell into something resembling love
at a tacky seaside resort. Shouldn't we fall out
of something resembling love
at a tacky seaside resort?

You Can't Say That

Thing is,
she was bored
with herself.
Bored with her life.
But you can't say that
on a first date.
So she said, "I love life.
I never know what's coming
next, and that's part of the thrill for me."

when drowning

you realize
the importance
of breathing

Donna

She sat awhile
looking at a speck of dust on her pantyhose.
Then she thought about heads
rotting on spikes.

turkey sandwich

hold the mayo
& mustard.
oh, ya got that fancy
dijon stuff?
yeah, no mustard.
your cranberry
sauce,
is it homemade?
it's made from scratch?
scratch
the cranberry sauce.
& no salt.
definitely no pepper.
y'know what?
hold the bread, please.
hold the turkey, too.

corrosion

the key
to your heart
snapped
in the lock

Snowfields

She's afraid
of being
afraid
of being alone
so she wears
her eyeliner thick
& cries out
& thinks:
white
while Tom
pounds
& pounds
& drenches her
in gin-heat
she thinks:
star flood
thinks: snowfields

Sad Professor

He's written everything
he knows about. Used up
his juice. And now
he's busy writing it all over again.

something under her arm

she ignored
the growth
because
she wasn't ready
for cancer

Fortune-Cookie Fortunes

When you hear prerecorded applause
take a bow.

They're coming in the night with their microchips.

Self-loathing is no longer in vogue.
Give yourself a hug.

Your heart's fucked (or you'll soon get cancer).
Forget retirement savings.

Guys fake orgasms too.

Never flush dead, or dying, goldfish
down the toilet.

You're too lazy for complete world domination.

Sure, you'll regret it.
But you'll regret not regretting it more.

Overdose at least once.

Collect something. Treasure your collection.
Then give said collection to the troll under the bridge.

Daddy doesn't forgive you.

Work

In movies and novels nobody seems to work.
I guess they wouldn't have time
to go on adventures and find themselves
and all if they had to work.

By Knife

Making love to a woman
While thinking about how
To best kill her husband.

Dancing Bear

I'll be your fierce bear in a vest
with little bells

I'll dance at the roadside
until my footpads scrape raw

until my flanks
are matted with dust & sweat

O put a ring in my nose
I'll dance I'll dance

put a shackle round my neck with a chain
I'll be your fierce bear in a vest

No Words

"This is the perfect moment"
can kill the moment.

Dear Liz

I don't know how
to say goodbye.
So I'm gonna stay.
Happy Birthday!

Why Does She Always Talk about Her Husband?

He breathes
heavily,
he rolls
over at least
seventy
times a night,
(she's counted),
he kicks,
he whimpers,
he shivers,
he chews on his pillow.

I ask her, What do I do in my sleep?

Nothing's New

The book was a flop. The marriage a tragedy.
The summer fierce and lonely. No. Just kidding.
Nothing's new, really. I was mostly busy with work
and I tried a yoga class—the type that incorporates
stretch poles and those balance ball things.
Oh, and we almost bought a new coffee maker.

Headache

I could feel a headache
coming on,
so I said, Forget it.
It's nothing. Don't worry about it.
Now, she says, I am worried.
Now I want you to tell me what it is.
You just can't do that to people.

Pyramid

When sand winds rage
and cut the eyes, I enter you.
I take nothing, leave nothing.
Shelter me tonight.

Car Wash

We had a car wash at our elementary school for Ricky,
a fifth grader, who had leukemia. We were raising money
for his parents to stay at a hotel right beside the children's
hospital in Vancouver. I was in sixth grade, and went with
mom and dad to help out at the car wash. There were about
ten of us washing cars, and we were all busy. People sort
of swapped duties, so no one got tired out by doing one thing.
It was my turn to handle the collection bucket—someone's
mom just handed it to me. "Your turn," she said. It was
a plastic ice-cream bucket with a slot cut into the lid. I felt
kind of important. I had control of the collection bucket for about
a minute when Ricky's mom came over and took it from me.
She didn't say anything. She just came up and took the bucket.

Consider

the once-cherished
people that
have vanished
from your life.
Is it easier
to think
of them as living
or dead?
I think of them as living.
That way, I don't need to think.

No Going Back

He got old. He decided
to get his teeth yanked out
and he got dental implants.
It was hard to eat with the implants.
It hurt to eat. He lost a lot
of the pleasure of eating.
He realized there was no going back.

isn't it actually

the more
you can hear

the quieter you become?

The Chair

A dentist
invented
the electric chair.
Isn't that
just perfect?

joe

in ninth grade
i thought
i was in love
with a twin

i liked brandi
(the slightly
introverted one)
her sister was
randi
(how perfect!)

but this story
isn't really
about the twins

this story
is about joe

joe attended
a creepy private
christian
school
where students
studied quietly
all day
in cubicles

so anyway
during
summer break
i show joe
a yearbook pic
of brandi
(the slightly
introverted twin
i thought
i was
in love with)

joe takes one look
at the pic & says
(grimly)
"seems like
the kinda girl
who masturbates
with a thermos"

goddamn
that turned me on!

A Kind of Trauma

My strongest memory of her
the one that trumps all others
is the way she looked in the coffin

Cream

She came to bed
with these dots
of cream on her face.
It was our first time
sharing a bed to sleep.
She told me to be careful
when I kissed her. Then, "Look, if you could
just not kiss me that would be better."

Marriage

I'm chained
at the ankles
to a slab of stone.
Otherwise it's Paradise.

Benefit of the Doubt

I've been trying to give people
the benefit of the doubt.
Like that cop sitting in his squad car
picking his nose. Hey, maybe the guy's on break.

Tiny Polka Dot Dress

Jane's gone quick for a couple packs of smokes
And a bottle.
She likes to joke, this one—
She said, "Don't you come looking for me—
I'm running off
With an old boyfriend
To Peru
And I'm changing my face."

She's back a little later than expected
With her dress on inside out.

Older

I always figured older people
had things figured out. They knew
what was what. Didn't question themselves.
They just knew and knew.
Not true.

Beth

I was in the hospital recovering for ten days after surgery.
My buddy and his wife, Beth, and baby girl came to visit me.
Beth handed me a basket of mandarin oranges. We all went down
to the cafeteria to get something to drink. Beth said she wanted
to come back and visit me again on Friday. That was in three days.
She'd bring the baby, she said. It gave her a reason to get out.
My buddy would be away at work. My buddy kind of made a face,
but then he seemed fine. After we finished our juice boxes, we got up.
My buddy shook my hand. Beth was holding the baby. I gave the baby
a slow, exaggerated wave. Beth gave me this hug with her free arm.
I couldn't sleep that night. Couldn't stop thinking about Friday.
I couldn't help thinking about the future. I would be well again.

The All-Important Question

Does he
Remove his
Wedding
Ring?
Or
(Fuck it!)
Does he
Leave it on?

kindly wait

for her to come
before you come

Double-Edged

It's good
because it fights
the cancer.
It's bad
because it fights
everything else as well.

Herbert the Empathy Toad

He told me
to fuck off and die

I'm sad

Next Big Thing

He Looks like a Pop Star
He Sounds like a Pop Star
He Is a Pop Star
Watch Him get Ripped Apart by Hyenas
Live Monday Night
Only on Pay-Per-View

End

She changed her glasses
and that changed everything.
He wanted her to go back
to those "perfect circle glasses."
She wouldn't go back.

Eight Line Poem

She put her things into
garbage bags and left
in the middle of the night.
Hitched a ride into the city.
She had breakfast.
Sat there with her garbage bags.
Then she called her husband.
Asked him to come and bring her home.

Redemption

Paradise, Utah. That's where he decides to go.
He's never been to Utah and he's never been
to Paradise. He wants to get away from his life
for a while. He wants to get away from his wife too.
He's hoping to start writing the novel that's been
on the backburner for at least seventeen years.
That novel about self-doubt and betrayal and sex
in South America (he's never been to South America).
So our hero gets to Paradise, Utah, and checks into
the Best Western for a week. He eats dinner,
reads a little, opens his hard covered notebook,
fiddles with some colored pens, and he misses
his wife. He badly wants to call her. But he told
his wife he needs this chance at silence, at freedom.
He told his wife he needs to see what he's made of.
He told his wife he's been stifled all these years
and writing the Book will redeem him. He calls his wife.

Widower's Poem

Pass the time.
Don't think too much.
Make a list of things
to pass the time.
Don't stand in the middle
of the room watching nothing.
Don't lie down in the middle
of the room in the middle
of the day.
Don't think too much.
Don't drift away.

Forgive

Anyway, I was just wondering if you could
forgive me for saying I wished you were never born.
I know I haven't apologized. But I'm hoping
you'll turn out to be the bigger person and maybe
let me off the hook for that. Thank you in advance.

Gabby

Name's Gabby, my friends call me
"Gerber Baby" (don't ask, you don't wanna know).
On better days, I feel about 47 years old.
I don't work, I don't really cook,
I've got poor sewing and laundry skills,
and I've developed a rare form of gum disease.
I don't like long walks on the beach.
I like sex with the TV turned up real loud.
I'm looking for hot, sizzling, True Love,
but I'll definitely settle for less.

Burnt Coffee

Drink up old friend
I've nothing more to offer

no brandy
no stirred silence &

no your lover's not been round
in her ragged muslin dress

drink up
it's already cold

After Festivities

Christmas tree
floating in the motel pool

Acknowledgements

These poems were published in the following literary magazines, to whose editors grateful acknowledgment is made.

The Antigonish Review: "tadpoles"
Cough Syrup Magazine: "kindly wait," "something under her arm"
The Dalhousie Review: "Tiny Polka Dot Dress," "turkey sandwich"
Dreich: "Benefit of the Doubt," "End," "Golden Ticket," "Longevity," "Marriage," "The End is the Beginning is the End," "Work"
Ellipsis: "Herbert the Empathy Toad"
Ethel Zine: "cactus juice"
Evening Street Review: "Beth"
Gargoyle Magazine: "Fortune-Cookie Fortunes," "Next Big Thing"
Glass Mountain: "Dad"
Hawaii Review: "Home"
Illuminations: "Burnt Coffee"
Into the Void: "joe"
MONO: "Forgive"
The Moth: "Gabby"
Mundane Joys (anthology): "the greed of weeds?"
The Nashwaak Review: "Wrong"
The North: "Jurassic Park"
North Dakota Quarterly: "After Festivities," "isn't it actually"
The Opiate: "corrosion," "Donna"
The Phoenix: "Double-Edged"
PN Review: "Freckles"
Poetry New Zealand: "Dancing Bear"
Poetry Salzburg Review: "Tina Says"
Popshot Quarterly: "Why Does She Always Talk about Her Husband?"
Shift: A Journal of Literary Oddities: "The Chair"
The Talon Review: "Cream"
Tower Poetry: "Widower's Poem"
Up the River: "Dear Liz"

Bio

David Romanda is the author of *I'm Sick of Pale Blue Skies*, a limited-edition chapbook, and *the broken bird feeder*, a full collection. His work has been included in *Best Canadian Poetry*. Romanda lives in Kawasaki City, Japan.

CPSIA information can be obtained
at www.ICGtesting.com
Printed in the USA
BVHW052253090223
658263BV00007B/354